Dynamite Crafts
for Special Occasions

FIRST EDITION
FIRST PRINTING

© 1993 by **TAB Books**.
TAB Books is a division of McGraw-Hill, Inc.

Library of Congress Cataloging-in-Publication Data

Lamancusa, Jim.
    Dynamite crafts for special occasions / by Jim Lamancusa.
     p.   cm.
    Includes index.
    ISBN 0-8306-4272-2
    1. Holiday decorations. 2. Handicraft. I. Title.
TT900.H6L36 1993
745.594'1—dc20   93-18548
                           CIP

Acquisitions Editor: Stacy Varavvas Pomeroy
Book Editor: April D. Nolan
Production team: Katherine G. Brown, Director
               Tina M. Sourbier, Coding
               Wanda S. Ditch, Layout
               Stephanie Myers, Computer Artist
               Tara Ernst, Proofreader
               Kristine D. Lively-Helman, Indexer
Design team: Jaclyn J. Boone, Designer
            Brian Allison, Associate Designer

KIDS

Contents

Dedication
This book is dedicated to my mom.
She is the most wonderful woman in the world.
She is there for me whether I win or lose.
She has helped me with this book so much.
Mom, I really love you. You are very special!

Acknowledgments
I would like to thank the following people for helping me complete this book:

My brother, Joe, for helping me with some of the projects

My aunt Kathy, for helping me with the instructions

And, always . . . my mother, for helping me with the projects and instructions.

Introduction

Whenever I look through kid crafting books, it is hard to find something that I want to do. Sometimes I think adults have no idea of what kids like to do. That's where I come in. This book will give fun projects to do for kids of all ages. The younger kids will learn shapes and colors, and the older kids can get ideas to entertain the younger ones. The majority of the projects are designed to be gifts, and you'll be surprised at how much positive recognition you will get from relatives and friends who receive your projects as presents.

Each part is filled with projects designed around a special holiday of the year. I begin the book with a Crafting Basics section, which shows you how to tie bows, curl ribbon, and clean and prepare shells. This section also includes tips and techniques of rubber stamping.

Part 1 is designed for New Year's and is great if you are planning a party. The chapter contains everything from party hats to noisemakers. Part 2 is for Valentine's Day. It is a good section to check out if you want to give someone something special to show them your love.

St. Patrick's Day isn't a widely celebrated holiday for craft projects, but Part 3 suggests a few ways you can promote the holiday. Part 4 is for spring and Easter. This chapter will give you a lot of fun projects to do at parties or alone. Part 5 is designed to give you ideas for a great many gifts for relatives. Sometimes we don't have the money to buy each of our relatives a gift, but this chapter will tell you how to make some quality gifts for your relatives.

In Part 6, you'll learn how to make some really fun projects to make over the summer vacation from school. You'll find a 4th-of-July project, decorated sunglasses, and projects that allow you to use the seashells you find at the beach. Part 7 kicks in when you are getting ready to go back to school. You always want to look your best when school starts, and this section will give you some easy and fun things to do to prepare for another year of classes.

I love Halloween, and in Part 8 you can find projects like masks, wearable art, and painted pumpkins. Part 9 is a fun one for fall and Thanksgiving. If you are an outdoors person, you'll find lots of things to use in this section. It includes a wreath, a decorated shirt, a turkey favor, and a placecard for Thanksgiving dinner. In Part 10, you'll find projects for Christmas and Hanukkah. This is a special time of the year, but sometimes we can't find the right decorations or gifts. Lots of ideas in this section will help you make gifts that are truly from the heart to share with your family and friends.

This book is so great because, being a kid myself, I know what kids really want to do. Sometimes parents think kids will enjoy something, but the kids might not want to do it. My book is useful for parents and teachers as well as kids. Parents can spend time with their kids, and both age groups can enjoy making the crafts.

After reading this book and trying several of the projects in it, you will have learned a great many new techniques for crafting. You'll get idea starters so that you can go on and design some of your own projects.

Crafting is special. You create items which can even become heirlooms as time goes on. But most importantly, the fun and enjoyment you will receive from creating and giving cannot be bought for any amount of money.

If you have any ideas for additional projects or would like to reach me with a problem or comment, you can write to me at McGraw-Hill. Enjoy!

Crafting basics

Here are a few crafting techniques that I have used throughout the book. You'll find them helpful for other projects you design on your own as well!

bow- ☆
making

The bow I have used is simple to create and can be used over and over again in many craft and creative projects. You can use any type or width of ribbon. Just follow the same directions, and all the bows will turn out great!

1. Cut a length of ribbon for the bow. (The length you need will be given in each of the projects.) If you are making a bow for yourself, measure how wide you want the bow to end up—let's say 5 inches (12.5 cm) as an example. Then double that figure because you will need a front and back to your bow. Our length is now up to 10 inches (25.5 cm). Then add 3 inches (7.5 cm) to 5 inches (12.5 cm) to the length (which is 10 inches (12.5 cm) in this example), depending on how wide the bow is. This is the part that you will overlap in this first step. So for our bow example you will cut the ribbon between 13 inches (32.5 cm) and 15 inches (38 cm) to start.
2. Bring the ends together, and overlap the ends approximately 1½ inches (4 cm) to 2½ inches (6.5 cm), depending on how wide the ribbon is. Follow the drawing below.
3. Bring the middle of the bow together. You will start to form your two loops, one on each side.

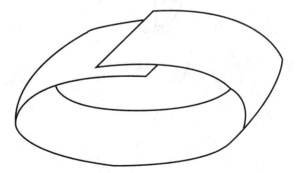 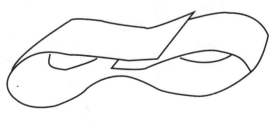

4. Pinch the ribbon together in the center. Now your two loops will be formed. The illustration will show you how.

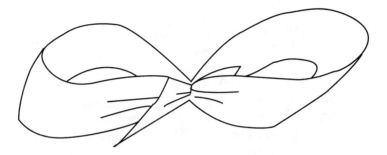

5. Wrap this center section with wire or tie it with ribbon to keep it together.

curling ☆ ribbon I have used a great deal of curling ribbon for the projects in this book. I really like the way it looks, and it is very inexpensive to buy. It also is very easy to curl, but be sure to ask an adult to help you with this.

1. Hold the ribbon as shown. Place the open end of a pair of scissors against a length of the ribbon, placing your thumb on top of the ribbon.

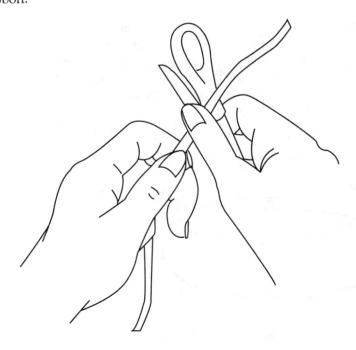

2. Pull the scissors and your thumb over the curling ribbon in a firm stroke. The ribbon will curl as it passes by the scissors.

rubber ☆ stamping

Using rubber stamps to create great projects is exciting and fun! Lists of the companies who provided me with products to do the stamping projects are in the back of the book. Look for these designs first; information is given on where and how to find the stamps used.

Even if you don't feel you can draw a straight line, you'll be able to make creative projects with a little practice of the techniques explained, mixed with some of your imagination.

These are the supplies you will need when creating rubber stamp projects. Not all of these are used on every project.

- ❏ Rubber stamps
- ❏ Rainbow ink pads
- ❏ Single-color ink pads
- ❏ Watercolor markers

If you wish to embellish your stamped designs you can do it with:

- ❏ Colored pencils
- ❏ Markers
- ❏ Brushes
- ❏ Paints
- ❏ Glitter
- ❏ Colored paper
- ❏ Paper punches in assorted shapes
- ❏ Sandpaper
- ❏ Sequins
- ❏ Beads
- ❏ Pom-poms
- ❏ Movable eyes
- ❏ Feathers
- ❏ Ribbon
- ❏ Fabric scraps
- ❏ Embroidery floss
- ❏ Stencils

The following are just a few things on which you can create rubber stamp designs:

- ❏ Paper
- ❏ Note cards
- ❏ Stationery
- ❏ Envelopes
- ❏ Bookmarks
- ❏ Stickers
- ❏ Puzzles
- ❏ Paper plates
- ❏ Paper cups
- ❏ Party hats
- ❏ Napkins
- ❏ Placemats
- ❏ Tablecloths
- ❏ Doilies
- ❏ Labels
- ❏ Gift tags

- ❏ Wrapping paper
- ❏ Tissue paper
- ❏ Cardboard
- ❏ Lunch bags
- ❏ Gift bags
- ❏ Balloons
- ❏ Shoes
- ❏ Shrink Art
- ❏ Wood

to stamp Select the stamp you would like to use, then tap it into the ink pad to get ink on it. If the stamp is larger, it will need more ink to print a clear design. Test your inked stamp on a piece of scrap paper first. Then gently reink the stamp. Carefully place the inked stamp onto the item you are stamping. Apply an even, firm pressure. Do not rock the stamp from side to side, or you might get a double image. Larger stamps will need a firmer pressure. Don't touch the finished stamped design until it is completely dry. Different designs need different drying times—don't get impatient!

markers You can use water-based markers to color directly onto the rubber stamp. This allows you to use several colors at once on the same rubber stamp. Simply color in the section you want with a marker, but be sure to use only water-based markers with this technique.

You will need to work quickly because the ink will dry in a short time. After applying the color you desire, quickly press the stamp onto the surface you are decorating.

coloring   You can color the design you have stamped onto your item. Stamp it in a solid color, then use markers, colored pencils, or paints to color in the sections of the stamp.

care & cleaning   To prevent muddy colors from appearing, always clean your stamps between colors and when you are through stamping. You can clean water-soluble stamp-pad inks with mild soap or window-washing solution. Special ink pad cleaners are also available. Solvent-based inks should be cleaned with denatured alcohol.

Stamp your stamp a few times on a clean piece of scrap paper to remove excess ink after stamping your designs. To use cleaners, moisten a paper towel with solution and wipe the stamp. Stamp on scrap paper again to remove residue. Use a toothbrush to remove ink stains which are difficult. Always store your stamps rubber side down and keep them out of direct sunlight.

seashells ☆   You can purchase pre-cleaned shells at most craft stores, but often it is fun to collect your own shells while at the beach during a vacation. When used in a craft project you create, seashells make a wonderful remembrance of a special vacation. Here are some tips on how to clean the shells you collect. Be sure to ask an adult for help.

empty shells Rinse the shells under tap water to remove sand and salt. After the shells are dry, bring out their natural beauty by using crystal clear glaze or mineral oil. Only use mineral oil on specimen shell.

starfish Place starfish in a solution of 9 parts water and 1 part formaldehyde. You can find formaldehyde in a pharmacy. Soak them for 24 hours and let dry.

cleaning shells To remove surface lime deposits (white film), green algae, brown skin layers, or barnacles on the shell, place the shells in full-strength bleach for about 1 hour. While wearing gloves, remove the shells and rinse them with water. Scrub the shells with a stiff vegetable brush. Repeat if necessary. You can remove difficult barnacles by prying them off with a knife and then sanding that location to remove the blemish. Apply crystal-clear glaze or mineral oil to bring out the beauty of the shell.

It is sometimes difficult to glue shells together. The best method I have found is to use Creatively Yours Clear Silicone from Loctite. It holds the shells well and isn't affected by temperature changes, which allows you to use the project outdoors or to store it in an attic.

Part 1
New Year's Eve

Every year, my family has a get-together on New Year's Eve. It has become a real tradition. We play games, cook a big meal, and make lots of noise to send the new year off to a great start. My brother and I like to make party favors and hats because they add a festive touch to the evening. Here are some projects that you might enjoy making next New Year's Eve. They'll send your new year off to a BANG!

1
Party hat

Party hats are fun to make and really can loosen people up to have fun. This one is especially easy to do with markers and rubber stamps. The more colorful, the better!

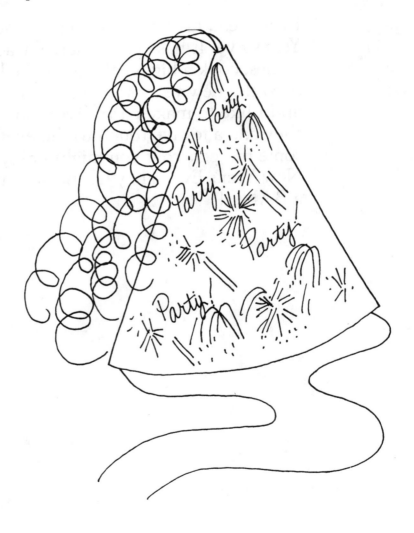

materials ☆ ❑ 18-inch-x-9-inch (45.5 cm × 22.5 cm) piece poster board for each hat
❑ Party rubber stamp
❑ Fireworks rubber stamp
❑ Felt markers: purple, red, blue, & green
❑ 4 yards (3.6 m) red curling ribbon
❑ 2 yards (1.8 m) green curling ribbon
❑ 2 yards (1.8 m) blue curling ribbon
❑ 2 yards (1.8 m) gold curling ribbon
❑ Glue
❑ Scissors
❑ Pencil

instructions ☆ 1. Ask an adult to help you transfer the hat pattern to your poster board. Then cut it out.

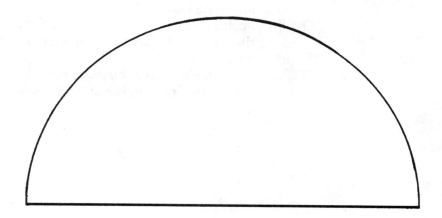

2. Color the fireworks stamp with the felt markers making each fireworks symbol a different color. (See the basics diagram on page xii for further explanation on this technique.) Stamp it onto the hat. Repeat, adding color and stamping to get an overall design on the poster board. Leave some open spaces for the Party stamp.
3. Color in the different letters of the Party stamp with the felt markers, and apply several stamps around the fireworks designs.
4. Roll the poster board into a cone shape and glue it in place.
5. Cut all the curling ribbon into lengths of 1 yard (.9 m) each.

6. Glue one end of a red piece of ribbon on the inside of the cone. Repeat with another length of ribbon directly across from the first one. These will be to tie the hat on.
7. Bring one end of all the other lengths of ribbon together and tie them all together with an overhand knot.
8. Grab the other ends of all of the ribbons in this bunch, and feed them through the inside of the hat to the outside through the point of the cone. If the hole isn't large enough, cut the tip of the cone off so you have more room. Don't cut too much or the ribbon knot will pull through; you want it to stay inside. Add a little glue to secure it.
9. Ask an adult to help curl the ribbon by running the blade of the scissors over each piece of ribbon. (See the basics diagram on page x for further explanation on this technique.)

tips ☆
❒ You could write the upcoming year number very large across the front of the hat.
❒ Glitter can make the hat really shine. Simply run a line of glue along the edge of the hat and sprinkle glitter on the glue. Let it dry before you wear it.
❒ This design makes a great birthday party hat. Or, if you add a brim and a row of ribbon, it instantly becomes a witch hat!

2
New Year's favor

With these three sacks, you have a ready-made party in your hand! One of the sacks is for the treat, the second is for the confetti, and the third is for the party streamers.

Filling the sacks is a two-person job, so ask someone to give you a hand with this project.

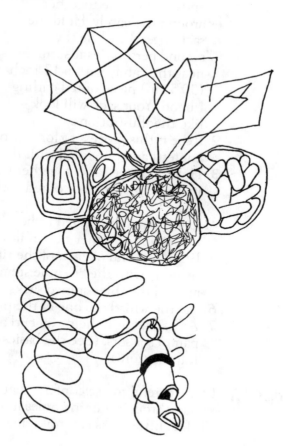

materials ☆

- ❏ Three 9-inch (22.5 cm) squares white nylon net or tulle
- ❏ Small amount of candy
- ❏ Small amount of confetti
- ❏ One roll of ¼-inch-wide (.6 cm) paper streamers
- ❏ 2 yards (1.8 m) red curling ribbon
- ❏ 1 yard (.9 m) gold curling ribbon
- ❏ 1 yard (.9 m) green curling ribbon
- ❏ 1 plastic whistle
- ❏ One 3-inch (7.5 cm) length white chenille stem or piece of cloth-covered wire
- ❏ Scissors

instructions ☆

1. Lay one square of tulle on the table. Place the candy in the center of the square. Bring the ends of the tulle together around the candy. Hold the sack together while the second person ties it securely near the candy with a 12-inch (30.5 cm) piece of red curling ribbon. Your sack will look like the illustrations.
2. Repeat this process to form two more sacks—one filled with confetti and one filled with the paper streamer.
3. Hold all three sacks together while the second person ties a 12-inch (30.5 cm) piece of red curling ribbon around all three sacks.
4. Cut the remaining red ribbon into two 12-inch (30.5 cm) pieces and all other ribbon into 18-inch (45.5 cm) pieces.
5. Bring one end of each of the ribbons together, and wrap them securely with the chenille stem. Then wrap the chenille stem around the three joined sacks.
6. Tie the whistle to one of the pieces of ribbon.
7. Ask an adult to help you curl all the ribbons with the blade of a pair of scissors. (See the basics diagram on page x for further information.)

tips: ☆

- ❏ Be careful to use confetti that has larger flakes so that it doesn't fall through the tiny holes in the net or tulle.
- ❏ The little sacks can hold small prizes for a birthday party.

3
Bell noisemaker

New Year's Eve is a time to make lots of noise in celebration. A simple noisemaker is easy to construct with a few bells and pieces of ribbon.

materials ☆
- ☐ Three or more 1-inch (2.5 cm) bells
- ☐ Two 3-inch (7.5 cm) pieces of chenille stem or cloth covered wire
- ☐ 1 yard (.9 m) gold curling ribbon
- ☐ 1 yard (.9 m) red curling ribbon
- ☐ 1 yard (.9 m) blue curling ribbon
- ☐ Scissors

instructions ☆
1. Cut each of the lengths of ribbon into three 12-inch (30.5 cm) pieces.
2. Bring one end of each ribbon together, and wrap this ribbon bunch with one piece of the wire.
3. Use the other wire to tie the three bells together.
4. Wire the ribbon cluster to the bells.
5. Ask an adult to help you curl all the ribbons with the blade of a pair of scissors. (See the basics diagram on page x for further information.)

tips ☆
- ☐ You can use any size or type of bell. The larger the bell, the sturdier the ribbon streamers should be.
- ☐ The bells also can be tied or glued onto the ribbon streamers if you like.
- ☐ Look around the house and see what other items you can string together to make a lot of noise!

4
Paper noisemaker

I used to make these noisemakers in school during recess because, when used, they make a big POP! Be careful of making them at school, though, because teachers really hate them, and you probably don't want to get into trouble the first thing when you get back to school for the new year.

materials ☆
- ☐ 8½-inch-×-11-inch (21.3 cm×28 cm) sheet white paper
- ☐ ⅝-inch (1.5 cm) rub-off letters in assorted neon colors
- ☐ ⅜-inch (.9 cm) rub-off letters in assorted neon colors
- ☐ ⅜-inch-wide (.9 cm) assorted-color stick-on stars
- ☐ ⅞-inch-wide (2 cm) assorted-color stick-on stars

instructions ☆ 1. Fold the paper in half longwise first, as shown in the illustration.
2. Next, fold the paper in half widthwise as shown.

3. Using the rub-off letters, form a message on the outside of one quarter of the paper. Use the message shown here, or design your own!
4. Stick the stars all around the message.
5. To use the noisemaker, hold it in your hand as shown, then rapidly snap it downward. It will make a BIG noise!

tips ☆ ❐ You can change the decoration on the front to say anything you want. If you are in a hurry, you can even use the noisemakers without a decoration.
❐ Use standard-weight paper, because if the paper is too heavy, it won't pop loudly.

Part 2
Valentine's Day

Valentine's Day is a great time to let someone know you think they are special, or just to say thank you for all that they do for you. Parents, grandparents, teachers, and special friends will love receiving these Valentine gifts.

5
Potpourri hearts

Potpourri hearts can be used as a decoration because they're pretty, or you can hang them in a small, enclosed area to make the room smell nice.

materials ☆
- [ ] 2 ounces (28.4 g) potpourri of your choice (I used Victorian Rose)
- [ ] 4-inch-wide (10 cm) heart shaped metal cookie cutter
- [ ] 1 yard (.9 m) ½-inch-wide pink picot-edged ribbon
- [ ] ½ yard (.5 m) ¼-inch-wide pink fused pearls
- [ ] Old nonreusable bowl (Don't use a good bowl or your mom will kill you!)
- [ ] Cooking spray
- [ ] Popsicle stick
- [ ] 6-inch square waxed paper
- [ ] Styrofoam cup
- [ ] Pencil
- [ ] White craft glue

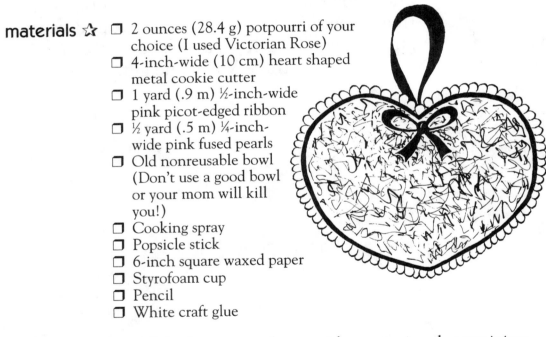

instructions ☆
1. Fill the foam cup to the top with potpourri, and empty it into the bowl.
2. Fill the cup ⅓ full of white craft glue, and then pour the glue into the bowl. It might seem like a lot, but you might even have to add more!
3. With your popsicle stick, mix the glue and the potpourri together. If it gets hard to mix, add more glue. It will probably

look like a big white mess, but don't worry; the glue will dry clearly.

4. Lightly spray the inside of the cookie cutter and the top of the waxed paper with cooking spray. Place the cookie cutter on the waxed paper.

5. When the potpourri and the glue are well-mixed and there are no big glue globs between the potpourri pieces, place the mixture into the cookie cutter. Don't be afraid to get your hands in it; the glue just rubs right off. With your fingers and the popsicle stick, press the mixture evenly in the cookie cutter. Make sure to fill in any holes.

6. Wait 15 minutes, but no longer—otherwise, the potpourri might stick to the cookie cutter, making it impossible to remove. Once you have removed it from the cookie cutter, place the potpourri heart on the waxed paper.

7. With a pencil, carefully poke a hole right below the V in the top of the heart.

8. Let the heart dry for 24 to 36 hours. Turn it over once in awhile so it will dry evenly.

9. When it is dry, spread glue all around the side of the heart. Stick the ribbon onto the glue, beginning and ending at the center top of the heart. Press ribbon in place for a minute or so. Cut off the extra ribbon.

10. Stick a 9-inch (22.5 cm) piece of ribbon through the hole so that there are equal amounts of ribbon on either side. Tie a knot on top of the heart, right in the V, so the ribbon is tight through the hole. Bring the two ends of the ribbon up and together. Tie the ends in a knot to form a loop.

11. Make a bow with 9 inches (22.5 cm) of ribbon, just like you tie your shoe. Glue this bow to the front of the heart. Cut the ribbon ends at a slant. Glue the string of pearls around the sides of the heart on top of the ribbon. Cut away any excess pearls.

tips ☆ ❏ Use smaller cookie cutters to make mini hearts. The mixture above will make two 2-inch (5 cm) hearts.
❏ Add a magnet to the back so the heart can be displayed on a refrigerator or on another piece of metal.
❏ Raid your mother's crafting boxes and use scraps of flowers, ribbons, and whatever else you can find to decorate the hearts. (Ask Mom first!)

6
Popsicle-stick treasure box

This box can be filled with candy or fancy little soaps (Moms and grandmas like those kinds of things). After the candy or soap is gone, they have a special gift left that they can fill with their favorite jewelry, make-up, or anything else they want to.

materials ☆
- [ ] Sixty popsicle sticks
- [ ] 4-inch (10 cm) round gold paper doily
- [ ] 6-inch (15 cm) red heart-shaped doily
- [ ] Four ⅝-inch (1.5 cm) red heart-shaped flat-backed beads

- ☐ Five ⅝-inch (1.5 cm) clear heart-shaped flat-backed beads
- ☐ ⅝-inch (1.5 cm) "U" wooden block
- ☐ ⅝-inch (1.5 cm) "I" wooden block
- ☐ Eight 1½-inch (4 cm) diamond mirror beads of assorted colors
- ☐ Red webbing spray
- ☐ White dimensional paint
- ☐ White craft glue

instructions ☆

1. Glue 11 popsicle sticks side by side and set them aside to dry. Repeat with 11 more popsicle sticks to form a second flat base.
2. Glue the gold doily on the center of one of the pieces you made in step 1. This will be the lid.
3. Cut the heart from the center of the red doily, and glue the heart on top of the gold doily.
4. Glue one red heart bead in each of the four corners of the lid.
5. Glue one of the clear hearts in the center of the paper heart.
6. Glue the "I" block on the left side of the clear heart, and glue the "U" block on the right side. Set the lid aside.
7. Glue two popsicle sticks on top of the alternate edges of the other base made in step 1, going in the opposite direction.
8. Glue two more popsicle sticks across the other two sides, gluing only the tips to the tips of the sticks placed in step 7.

9. Repeat step 7 with two more sticks, again gluing only the tips.
10. Repeat step 8. Continue gluing two popsicle sticks at a time on opposite sides until all the sticks are used up.
11. Glue one clear heart in the center on all four sides of the box.
12. Glue one diamond on each side of the hearts.

13. Following the diagram, cut a heart shape from paper and lay it on the bottom of the box.

14. Spray the webbing over the rest of the box.
15. Remove the paper heart, and outline the heart shape with white dimensional paint.

7
Candy holder

This project is really quick and easy to make. Fill it with wrapped candies or other special treats. It would make a great teacher's gift. It is soft and pretty because of the paper doily, but you could make it out of colored construction paper.

materials ☆
- ☐ One 8-inch (20 cm) round, white paper-lace doily
- ☐ One 6-inch (15 cm) heart-shaped, red, paper-lace doily (you can spray-paint a white one)
- ☐ 5-inch (12.5 cm) circle poster board
- ☐ 2 yards (1.8 m) white yarn
- ☐ Glue
- ☐ Inexpensive paintbrush, chenille stem, or popsicle stick (to apply glue)
- ☐ Silver glitter
- ☐ Paper hole punch

instructions ☆
1. Center the red heart doily on top of the round white doily. (Try to match up the openings.)
2. Punch a series of holes down each side of the heart with both layers of doilies together. This will create the holes to weave the yarn through.
3. With the white yarn, start at the bottom point of the heart and weave the two doilies together. Leave about 6 inches (15 cm) of yarn hanging loose from where you start your weaving.
4. Weave along one side of the heart, leaving the top of the heart open to insert candy. Then weave down the other side of the heart and end at the bottom point. Leave 12 inches (30 cm) of the yarn loose at the top of the heart. You can use this excess yarn to hang the heart, or you can tuck the yarn inside, between the two doilies.
5. Tie the two ends of yarn together at the point of the heart to form a bow. This bow should be tied just like you tie your shoe. Cut off any extra yarn.
6. Using an inexpensive paintbrush, a popsicle stick, a chenille stem, or your finger, apply glue all around the outside edge of the round doily.
7. Sprinkle the silver glitter on the glued areas. Shake off the excess. Allow this to dry, and then fill the heart with candy or other treats of your choice.

8
Stained-glass suncatcher

This suncatcher would be a great gift for Dad or Grandpa. They could hang it on their office window. You can create your own message or design after reading through our instructions so that you understand the process of creating stained-glass-looking projects.

❐ 5-inch-×-7-inch (12.5 cm×17.5 cm) Suncatcher frame or piece of heavy plastic

❐ Antique bronze liquid leading

❐ Pencil

❐ Tracing paper

❐ Paintbrush

instructions ☆

1. If you are creating your own design, draw a rectangle 5 inches × 7 inches on a piece of paper. Draw your design or message on the paper, keeping within the outline. Be sure you have areas which will hold additional colors. For example, notice the "I" in the pattern we drew. It is not just printed to look like an "I," it has been outlined so that color could be added in the center and the leading will trap the color in.

2. If you want to use our design, simply place the tracing paper on top of the pattern in the book and trace it.

3. Place the suncatcher on top of the tracing paper. Tape the pattern to the form to keep it from shifting while you work.

4. Protect the work area with newspaper. Keep your work area level.

5. Practice drawing some leading lines first on newspaper.

6. With the liquid leading, trace the design onto the suncatcher. Hold the tip of the bottle about ½ (1.3 cm) inch from the suncatcher surface. Use constant, even pressure and a slow, continuous motion. Work from the top to the bottom. You can correct mistakes with a toothpick or a cotton swab as long as the leading is still wet.

7. Let the leading dry 3 to 4 hours or overnight before applying glass stain.

8. Make sure your working surface is level so the glass stain will spread evenly.

9. Apply the glass stain with a brush or directly from a squeeze bottle.

10. Use assorted colors to finish your design.

11. Allow the stain to dry 4 to 5 hours or overnight in a normal room temperature.

tips ☆

❐ You can order liquid leading and the suncatcher from Kelly's Crafts. Refer to the mail-order section in the back of the book for ordering information.

Part 3
St. Patrick's Day

We all have some Irish friends. Wouldn't it be nice to surprise them with a special St. Patrick's Day decoration that was made especially with them in mind? But looking at it differently, we are all Irish on St. Pat's Day—so make one for yourself, too!

$\mathcal{9}$
Shamrock paint sticker

You can use this sticker to decorate mirrors, windows, refrigerators, and any other smooth, slick surface. It is very easy to make and you can use the same technique for other holidays, too.

materials ☆
- ❏ 4-inch (10 cm) square piece of glass
- ❏ Dark-green dimensional paint
- ❏ Light-green dimensional paint

instructions ☆

1. Place the sheet of glass on top of the pattern shown here, and outline the shamrock with the dark-green paint.
2. Fill in with the light-green paint.
3. Let dry overnight. In the morning, you'll be able to peel it off of the glass and use it to decorate smooth, slick surfaces such as windows, lunch boxes, binders, and more!

tips ☆
- ❏ Be careful not to put too much pressure when removing the stickers. The corners of the paint may split. To repair, simply place back on the original piece of glass. Then add more paint to the crack and let the repair it dry overnight.

10
Shamrock button

Making different kinds of buttons is really fun. A shamrock is easy to make and could really be worn all the time for good luck.

materials ☆
- ❏ 2½-inch (6.5 cm) two-part plastic button
- ❏ Dark-green dimensional paint
- ❏ Gold glitter dimensional paint

instructions ☆

1. Take the two parts of the button apart. Set the back aside. Turn the front over, and place on top of the shamrock pattern. The cupped side of the front of the button should be facing you. The actual front of the button will be facing down on the pattern.
2. Using the green paint, fill in the entire shamrock shape. Let the paint dry overnight.
3. Turn the front of the button over. With the gold glitter paint, outline the shamrock shape and write ST. PAT'S in the center of the shamrock. Let this dry overnight.
4. Put the front and back of the button together again.

11
Luck-o'-the-Irish card

Greeting cards are always fun to receive, but they can be even more fun to make. Use the techniques described for this St. Patrick's Day card to make cards for other holiday seasons.

Here's some Irish luck for you...

materials ☆

- ☐ 4½-inch-×-6-inch (11.3 cm×15 cm) blank white greeting card with envelope
- ☐ 4½-inch-×-6-inch (11.3 cm×15 cm) piece white paper
- ☐ Green fine-tip marker
- ☐ "Bag" rubber stamp
- ☐ Gold ink pad
- ☐ Green and gold shamrock-shaped confetti
- ☐ Two 3-inch-×-6-inch (7.5 cm×15 cm) pieces clear cellophane
- ☐ Utility blade or fine manicure scissors

instructions ☆

1. Stamp an impression of the bag in the center of the front of the card near the bottom.
2. Ask an adult for help in this next step. I you will be using a utility blade, open the card and place the front on a piece of corrugated cardboard or a cutting mat. I you're using manicure scissors, hold the card while cutting.
3. Cut around the bag as shown in the diagram. You will be removing this entire piece. Cut a slit across the top of the bow as shown by the dotted line.

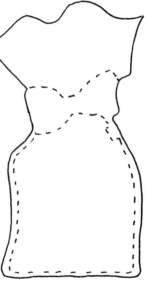

4. Turn the card over. Lay one piece of cellophane over the hole. Glue the bottom down even with the bottom of the bag cutout.
5. Pull the top of the bag through the slit to the front of the card.
6. Place the shamrock confetti on top of the cellophane in the center of the hole. Glue the second piece of cellophane over the confetti, gluing all around the cut edge. This will lock the shamrocks inside the bag.
7. Glue the 4½-inch-×-6-inch (11.3 cm ×15 cm) piece of paper over this section of the card to hide everything that was done here.
8. Turn the card over. Write your message with the green marker.
9. Glue random shamrocks around the card placing a few on the edge of the envelope.

Part 4
Spring & Easter

Bright-colored pom-poms, felt, and ribbon help to
create these Easter and spring projects. They
make great decorations and even better gifts. All
you have to do to make them complete is add the
fun.

12
Bunny magnet

Wouldn't you love to have a project you made displayed on the refrigerator throughout the season and maybe even all year? This is a perfect project to give as a gift for Easter.

materials ☆

- ❏ 5-inch (12.5 cm) square pink felt
- ❏ 2-inch (5 cm) square white felt
- ❏ One 1½-inch (4 cm) white pom-pom
- ❏ Two ½-inch (1.3 cm) white pom-poms
- ❏ One ⅜-inch (.9 cm) pink pom-pom
- ❏ Two ⅝-inch (1.5 cm) oval movable eyes
- ❏ 5-inch (12.5 cm) square poster board
- ❏ Glue
- ❏ ½-inch (1.3 cm) magnet strip or circular magnet
- ❏ Scissors
- ❏ Tracing paper

instructions ☆

1. Trace the pattern onto the tracing paper, and then onto the piece of poster board. Cut it out.
2. Glue this piece of poster board to the pink felt square.
3. When the glue is dry, cut the felt away around the poster board pattern.
4. Glue the 1½-inch (4 cm) pom-pom into the center of the circle on the felt side.

5. Glue the two ½-inch (1.3 cm) white pom-poms next to each other on the lower half of the large white pom-pom.

6. Glue the ⅜-inch (.9 cm) pink pom on top of the two small poms.

7. Glue the two eyes above the two white ½-inch (1.3 cm) pom-poms.

8. Transfer the pattern for the center of the ears to the white felt, and cut out two pieces.

9. Glue these two pieces to the center of the ears of the bunny.

10. Glue the magnet to the poster-board back of the bunny.

13
Bunny puzzle

Most kids love putting puzzles together. It's even more fun to make your own. You can make these as a gift for a younger brother or sister for any holiday or occasion.

materials ☆
- ☐ 5½-inch-×-4-inch (13.8 cm × 10 cm) blank puzzle card with envelope or piece, or poster board the same size
- ☐ 2½-inch-tall (6.5 cm) Easter basket rubber stamp
- ☐ Egg rubber stamp with three ½-inch (1.3 cm) eggs
- ☐ 2½-inch-tall (6.5 cm) bunny rubber stamp
- ☐ Grass-cluster rubber stamp
- ☐ Sun rubber stamp 1½ inch (4 cm)

- ❒ Colored markers
- ❒ Brown stamp pad or brown marker
- ❒ Green stamp pad or green marker

instructions ☆

1. Prepare the brown basket either by pressing it in the brown ink pad or by coloring the back of the stamp with the brown marker. Place the stamp on the left side of the puzzle.
2. Do the same with the bunny, placing him on the right side of the puzzle.
3. Color the back of the eggs stamp in different colors. Place the egg stamp inside the basket.
4. Color the back of the sun stamp orange, red, and yellow. Place the sun in the sky.
5. Make lots of grass cluster stamp impressions at the base of the puzzle, overlapping the bunny and basket. Use the green ink pad or a green marker.
6. Color the egg stamp in with different-colored markers, and place the impression on the outside of the envelope.

tips ☆

- ❒ If you can't find the puzzle shapes, you can do the design on poster board, then cut it up into puzzle pieces.

14
Easter basket

This project would make a pretty table decoration. It is very bright and colorful. Fill it with Easter eggs or candy.

materials ☆
- [ ] 12-inch-wide (30.5 cm) × 12-inch-tall (30.5 cm) basket
- [ ] 1⅓ yard (1.2 m) 2½-inch-wide (6.5 cm) yellow gathered lace
- [ ] 1½ yard (1.3 m) ¼-inch (.6 m) pink fused pearls
- [ ] Four 9-inch (22.5 cm) lengths of precurled ribbon in assorted pastel colors
- [ ] 1½ yards (1.3 m) 3-inch-wide (7.5 cm) sheer striped ribbon
- [ ] Iridescent Easter grass to fill basket
- [ ] Three 2-inch (5 cm) plastic eggs in assorted colors
- [ ] Glue
- [ ] Three 3-inch (7.5 cm) lengths white chenille stem or cloth-covered wire
- [ ] Items to fill basket

instructions ☆
1. Glue the lace trim around the edge of the basket.
2. Glue the fused pearls around the basket edge on top of the lace trim.
3. Cut the sheer ribbon into three 18-inch (45.5 cm) lengths. Form two of these lengths into a basic cylinder bow as shown in the Basics section (page ix). Secure each bow with a length of wire.
4. Fold the third length in half and wrap it around the center with one of the wire lengths.
5. Put the two cylinders side by side and the streamers below, and twist all wires together.
6. Glue the bow to the front of the basket at the base of the handle.
7. Remove any stems on the eggs, and glue them into the center of the bow.
8. Fill the basket with Easter grass.

15
Shell Easter bunny

You can make this great project with those seashells you collected at the beach last summer. It is fun to create, and you can make many in different colors to use as decorations. To prepare your shells, read the basic instructions for shells in the Basics section at the beginning of the book.

materials ☆
- ☐ Five 2-inch (5 cm) scallop shells
- ☐ One 1-inch (2.5 cm) cowrie shell
- ☐ Six purple bump chenille pieces
- ☐ Two ½-inch (1.3 cm) movable eyes
- ☐ One ¼-inch (.6 cm) red pom-pom
- ☐ 1¼-inch-wide (3.1 cm) premade polka-dot satin bow
- ☐ One ¾-inch (1.8 cm) purple ribbon rose
- ☐ Clear silicone or crafter's cement

instructions ☆
1. Glue two scallop shells together, back to back, as shown. Repeat, but take a two-bump length of bump chenille and fold it in half. Repeat to form a second one. Insert these between the shells on the rounded side to form bunny ears.
2. Glue these two scallop shell sections from step 1 together, end to end, to create head and body. Allow this to dry.
3. Glue the cowrie shell near the back of the curved portion of the fifth scallop shell. Let this dry.
4. Glue the shells from step 2 vertically onto the shell from step 3, resting the base against the cowrie shell for support. The ears

should be at the top. Prop this up, and let it dry.

5. Glue on the wiggle eyes, red pop-pom nose, and bow as shown in the drawing.

6. Cut two remaining bump-chenille pieces into single pieces. Cut off ¼ of each bump, and glue this to the base as feet. Glue the remaining portion of the bump chenille between the body shells as arms.

Part 5
Gifts for relatives

Handmade gifts are filled with love. The time spent making the gift is also filled with thoughts of pleasing the person we are going to give it to. Because of this, gifts for relatives are extra special. Sometimes it is even possible to get yourself out of trouble by making a gift for the person you have angered to show how sorry you are and how much you care about them.

16
Doorknob hangers

A little imagination, rubber stamps, and stickers are the main ingredients for this project. This project would be a fun gift to give your friends or to surprise your little brother or sister.

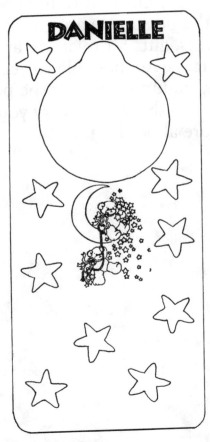

Design © Lucy Rigg

Design © 1992 Posh Presents
© 1992 Warner Bros., Inc.
© Hampton Art Stamps

materials ☆ ❏ Blank doorknob hanger
❏ Your choice of rubber stamps (we used a teddy bear, moon, and stars on one of the designs and spiders, webs, the Tasmanian Devil, paintbrushes, and Party stamps on the other
❏ "Name" rubber stamps of your choice
❏ Hologram star sequins
❏ Assorted colors brush markers
❏ Assorted color stamp pads

instructions ☆ 1. See our drawings for the placement of the indicated stamps. Follow our examples, or use your own imagination.
2. Read all the basics of rubber stamping in the Basics section at the beginning of this book.
3. Relax and have fun!

17
Gift wrapping

Once you have created a great gift, you can use these ideas to package it in a really fun way.

Monster ☆
bag

This monster gift bag is so great, it's almost enough of a gift by itself.

materials ☆
- ❏ 8-inch-x-10-inch (20 cm × 25.5 cm) plain yellow gift bag with rigid stand-up handles
- ❏ 6-inch (15 cm) square neon yellow felt
- ❏ 4-inch (10 cm) square neon green felt
- ❏ 4-inch (10 cm) square neon pink felt
- ❏ 8-inch (20 cm) square purple felt
- ❏ 8-inch (20 cm) square neon orange felt
- ❏ 6-inch (15 cm) square white felt
- ❏ 6-inch (15 cm) square cardboard or poster board
- ❏ Two 1-inch (2.5 cm) wiggle eyes
- ❏ Black felt marker
- ❏ Two spring-curly shoelace ties, assorted colors
- ❏ Silicone glue
- ❏ Craft glue

instructions ☆

1. Following the pattern, cut two of the larger eye circles from yellow felt. Cut the same two from poster board.

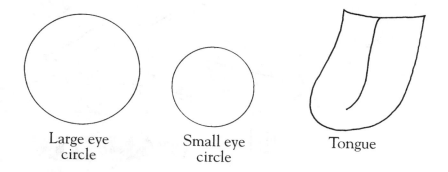

Large eye circle   Small eye circle   Tongue

2. Using craft glue, attach the two felt circles to the two poster board circles.
3. Cut the two smaller eye circles from green felt. Set aside.
4. Glue the two large yellow felt circles attached to poster board to the top edge of the bag handles, side by side.
5. Twist one shoelace tie on either side of the handle, gluing one end to the edge of the bag and the other to the back of the eye circle.
6. Glue one green felt circle to each yellow circle, with one toward the top and the other toward the bottom.
7. Glue one wiggle eye in each green circle.

8. Draw a crazy, wiggly mouth on the front of the bag.

9. Using the pattern, cut a tongue from the pink felt and glue it under the mouth. By gluing only along the top edge and placing a large, candy-kiss-sized glob of silicone under the bottom of the tongue piece, you can make the mouth stand away from the bag, adding a bit of dimension.

10. Cut different-sized patches from the purple and orange felt, and glue them all over the bag with the craft glue.

11. Cut four small, white, funny-shaped teeth from the white felt, and glue two on each side of the tongue.

Basic box ☆ Here is another great gift wrapping idea that your cousins or friends will be sure to enjoy!

materials ☆
- [ ] One white gift box
- [ ] Micky Mouse and balloon rubber stamp
- [ ] Single-balloon rubber stamp
- [ ] Name (of your choice) rubber stamp
- [ ] Black stamp pad
- [ ] Neon stamp pad
- [ ] Rainbow-colored felt-tip markers
- [ ] ¾-yard (.8 m) iridescent paper ribbon
- [ ] 3-inch (7.5 cm) length white chenille stem
- [ ] Glue

instructions ☆
1. Apply a stamp of Mickey with black ink to the center front of the box.
2. Color the stamp in with different colors of markers.
3. Apply the name once to the front of the box and several times around the sides with neon-colored stamp-pad ink.
4. Stamp single balloons around the box sides with neon-colored ink.
5. Draw balloon strings with markers.
6. Form a bow with the iridescent ribbon. Follow the directions for a cylinder bow in the Basics section at the front of this book. Make the first cylinder with ½ yard (.5 m) of ribbon and the center cylinder with 6 inches (15 cm) of ribbon. Secure with the chenille stem and glue to the top of the box.

tips ☆
- [ ] See the stamping instructions in the Basics section at the front of this book for more stamping details.

18
High-flying Dad kite

Tell Dad he is a really special guy with this very impressive kite project. Surprise him one morning by hanging it above his place at the table before breakfast or near his favorite chair. Of course, you can use this idea for Mom, too—or any other relative you want to impress!

materials ☆
- [ ] 14-inch (35 cm) square foam board or heavy cardboard
- [ ] 18-inch (45.5 cm) square yellow felt
- [ ] 1 yard (.9 m) ⅜-inch-wide red double-faced satin ribbon
- [ ] 1 yard (.9 m) metallic blue twisted-paper ribbon
- [ ] 2-inch-tall (5 cm) alphabet stencils
- [ ] Thirteen 3-inch (7.5 cm) squares assorted colors of felt
- [ ] Heavy black felt-tip marker
- [ ] Craft glue
- [ ] String

instructions ☆
1. Lay the square of felt on a table. Center the square of foam board on top of the felt. You should be able to see about 2 inches of felt all around the board.
2. Bring the edges of one side of the felt around to the back of the board and glue the felt to the board. Repeat, bringing all four sides of felt to the back and gluing them in place.

3. Glue one end of the red ribbon to the bottom point of the back of the square. Overlap the ribbon and board approximately 2 inches (5 cm).
4. Cut the twisted-paper ribbon into 5-inch (12.5 cm) pieces. Untwist each piece.
5. Pinch in the center of each 5-inch (12.5 cm) piece. Glue the first piece of pinched ribbon to the red ribbon, a few inches below the kite.
6. Continue gluing these pieces, equally spaced, down the ribbon.
7. One by one, draw the letters of your message on each of the squares of felt. To do this, simply center that particular stencil letter on the square of felt, and color it in with the black marker.
8. Cut all around the letter, leaving a small amount of colored felt showing around the letter. Leave each letter in one piece. Do not cut apart at each break in the stencil.
9. Glue the message to the front of the kite, and hang with a string glued to the back.

19
Picture frame

What Mom or Dad, grandma or grandpa, favorite aunt, uncle, or godparent wouldn't love this gift? Include a picture of you when you were doing something fun with the person you are giving it to. That would be extra-special.

materials ☆ ❏ One incredibly cute photograph of you or of you and the person you are giving it to
❏ Ten 4½-inch (11.3 cm) popsicle sticks
❏ Four ½-inch (1.3 cm) red rhinestone heart beads with flat backs
❏ Two ⅜-inch (.9 cm) white acrylic beads

□ Two ⅜-inch (.9 cm) pink acrylic beads
□ Craft glue

instructions ☆

1. Glue four popsicle sticks together to form a square. Allow ¼ inch (.6 cm) of each popsicle stick to extend beyond the one it is glued to.

2. Glue two more popsicle sticks on top of the four that are forming a square. Make sure these are positioned a little closer to the center. Approximately half of the popsicle stick underneath it should be showing.

3. Glue two more sticks in the same manner, but on opposite sides of the square.

4. Glue four more popsicle sticks, following the directions in steps 2 and 3. You should end up with an opening 1¼-inch-×-2¾ inch. Allow the frame to dry.

5. Glue the picture to the back of the frame. Trim if necessary.

6. Glue four red flat-back rhinestone beads to the four center corners of the picture frame.

7. Glue the four beads to the outside corners of the frame. Allow to dry.

20
Coupons

This coupon good for 1 HUG! HUG HUG HUG HUG HUG	This coupon good for CLEANING THE CAR!
I will spend tonight with you (instead of watching TV)! play games read stories take a walk play catch	This coupon good for 4 hours of BABYSITTING!
I will wash and dry the dinner dishes (without complaining)!	I will wash, dry, fold and put away this week's laundry. (and I'll do it right!)

materials ☆ ☐ Pieces of paper—any kind or size will work
☐ Rub-off letters or markers to write your own message

instructions ☆ Here are a number of different styles of coupons you could create. Use your imagination, and I know you'll think of a lot more!

21
Stamped cards

Ever have a problem finding a card with just the right message?
Create your own and the problem is solved. These designs can be
used for greeting cards, invitations, thank-you notes, and a whole
lot more.

materials ☆
- ☐ Paper, cards, envelopes—all in sizes and types of your choice
- ☐ Assorted rubber stamps
- ☐ Assorted-colored markers
- ☐ Assorted-colored stamp pads

instructions ☆ You can make so many different types of cards that I have just
tried to get you started with some ideas. Read the stamping basics
in the Basics section in the beginning of this book. It will give you
all the background information you need. Then just take a look at
what I have created and use it as an example of what you can do.

Design © Hampton Art Stamps

Design © Hampton Art Stamps

Design © Hampton Art Stamps

Design © 1992 Posh Presents
© 1981-1992 Suzy Spafford

Start the new year off with a bang by making these great crafts, including hats, noisemakers, and party favors.

What better way to show someone you love them than by giving them a Valentine's Day gift you made yourself? Potpourri hearts, treasure boxes, candy holders, and suncatchers are sure to warm the hearts of family and friends.

Wearable crafts provide double the fun because after you make them, you can wear them! (Left) Celebrate July 4th with the flag shirt or the coming of fall with this unique leaf shirt. (Below) Going back to school dosen't have to be a bore...make your own sweatshirts and book bag and start the year off right.

The coming of spring is sure to bring out your creativity. Celebrate with St. Patrick's Day and Easter crafts— cards, baskets, stickers, and more!

Summer vacation from school is the best time for kid crafting. Make your own firecrackers, travel games, and sunglasses— or find a unique way to use seashells from your trip to the beach.

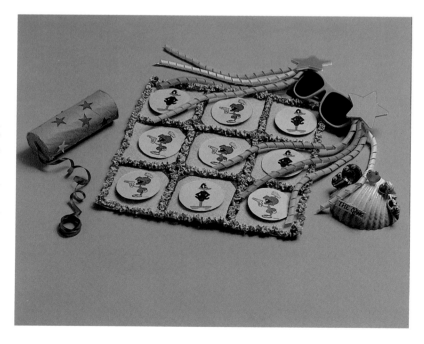

Halloween crafts are "boo-tiful" fun! You can make masks, hats, cards, and even a fuzzy spider.

What better way to close out the year than with Christmas crafts? You can make a reindeer visor, as well as lots of different Christmas and Hanukkah ornaments.

Part 6
Summer vacation

Summertime is always great fun. No school is something we all look forward to, but then often, once we are in the middle of the summer, we get really bored. Parents get upset when we constantly complain about the lack of things to do. This summer, instead of complaining, get started on many of the ideas in this section. It will keep your mind occupied and hands busy. Besides, it's a lot of fun!

22
Firecracker

This is a perfect party decoration for the 4th of July. Not only can you use it as a decoration, but you also can make several and pass them out as favors filled with candy or treats.

materials ☆
- ❏ Toilet paper roll
- ❏ 6-inch (15 cm) square red tissue paper
- ❏ Two 2-inch (5 cm) squares red tissue paper
- ❏ Sixteen ¾-inch-wide (1.8 cm) stick-on stars in assorted colors
- ❏ 1 yard (.9 m) royal-blue curling ribbon

❏ Glue
❏ Scissors

instructions ☆

1. Place the end of the toilet-paper roll on one of the squares of tissue paper. Trace the circular end of the roll. Cut out with scissors. Repeat to form a second circle. Set these aside.
2. Roll the toilet paper roll on the 6-inch (15 cm) square of tissue paper until it is completely covered. Glue the ends of the tissue paper. Trim away any excess paper from the ends of the roll.
3. Place a ring of glue around the ends of the toilet paper roll, and attach the two circles you cut previously.
4. Curl the ribbon by running the blade of the scissors over the ribbon. Ask an adult to help out here.
5. Glue one end of the ribbon to one end of the toilet paper roll. Place a star over the end.
6. Use the rest of the stars to decorate the sides of the firecracker.

tips ☆

❏ These are great to use to decorate the picnic table on the 4th of July. You also could fill them with surprises or treats before gluing the circles over the ends and give one to each person who attends your holiday party.

❏ Instead of a ribbon streamer, cut the shape of a candle flame from yellow construction paper and glue the flame to the end of the roll. Use this "candle" to decorate at Christmas or to fill with treats.

23
Flag shirt

Wear the red, white, and blue to show how much America and its flag mean to you. This shirt is colorful and really fun to wear.

materials ☆
- [ ] One white T-shirt, washed without fabric softener
- [ ] 2-inch (5 cm) wide masking tape
- [ ] ½-inch-wide (1.3 cm) masking tape
- [ ] Red floral spray dye
- [ ] Blue floral spray dye
- [ ] T-shirt form or piece of cardboard to put in shirt while painting
- [ ] Thirty star-shaped flat-backed beads ½ inch wide (1.3 cm)
- [ ] Fabric glue
- [ ] Newspaper

instructions ☆
1. Using the 2-inch (5 cm) masking tape, tape off a square of the shirt in the upper left corner as shown in the illustration. This is for the blue field of the flag.
2. Place 2-inch (5 cm) strips of masking tape 2 inches (5 cm) apart over the rest of the shirt). These will represent the stripes of the flag.
3. Place the taped shirt on top of lots of newspaper, and do the next steps outside or in a well ventilated area. Tape a piece of newspaper on top of the whole shirt, leaving the section

54 Dynamite Crafts for Special Occasions

in step 1 open as shown in the drawing. You are doing this so that no blue paint will reach the stripes.

4. Shake the can of paint well, then hold it 12 inches (30.5 cm) to 18 inches (45.5 cm) away from the shirt and entirely spray the exposed shirt with blue paint in slow, even, back-and-forth strokes. It is best to ask your parents to help with the painting. Let this section of the shirt dry.

5. Remove the newspaper covering the shirt. Move the tape you put on in step 1 so that it falls on top of the edge of blue instead of next to it. If you don't do this, you will have a white line around the blue section instead of having the red stripes next to it. Also, be sure that the 2-inch (5 cm) tape strips go all the way up to the blue section.

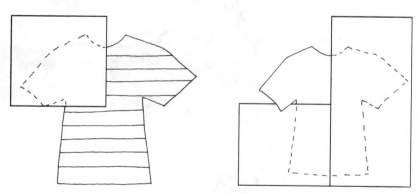

6. Cover the entire blue section with newspaper so that no red paint has a chance to run into the blue section.

7. Follow the directions in step 4 and spray the stripes with red paint. Allow this to dry completely

8. Remove all newspaper and masking tape.

9. Glue the 30 stars all over the blue section any way you would like.

tips ☆ ❏ I used Design Master Color Tool sprays in this project. This is important because other spray paints will make the fabric stiff.

24
Girl's sunglasses

Sunglasses are fun to wear all summer. But the best part about it is that you can look really cool if you design your own sunglasses. Everyone will want to know where you got them!

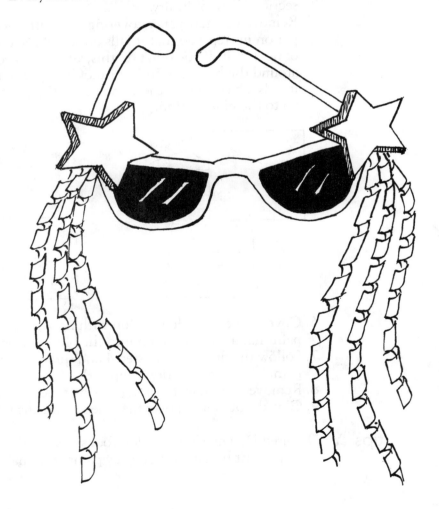

materials ☆
- ☐ Sunglasses
- ☐ Two 4-inch (10 cm) squares neon-colored poster board or foam board
- ☐ Eight 12-inch (30.5 cm) lengths precurled ribbon in assorted colors
- ☐ Glue
- ☐ Sharp scissors for cutting poster board or X-Acto knife for cutting foam board

instructions ☆
1. Trace patterns for the two stars, provided here, onto the poster board or foam board. Cut out the stars. Be sure to ask your parents to help with the cutting.
2. Put the ends of four of the lengths of curled ribbon together and glue at one corner of the glasses. Glue the other four lengths on the other corner of the glasses.
3. Glue one star over the ends of the curled ribbon at each corner of the glasses.

25
Boy's sunglasses

You can mix and match the lightning bolts from this design with the stars from the girl's design and create some designs of your own. Match the colors of the decorations with the colors of the sunglasses you select.

materials ☆
- ❏ Sunglasses
- ❏ One 12-inch (30.5 cm) length chenille stem
- ❏ Three different colors squeeze-on paint
- ❏ 5-inch (12.5 cm) square neon-colored poster board or foam board
- ❏ One ½-inch (1.3 cm) movable eye
- ❏ Glue
- ❏ Sharp scissors to cut poster board or X-Acto knife to cut foam board

instructions ☆ 1. Trace the patterns for the two lightning bolts onto poster board or foam board. Ask your parents for help cutting these out.

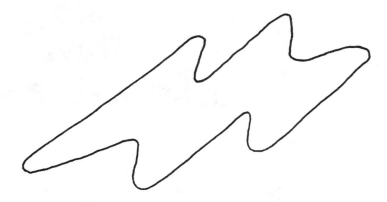

2. Cut the chenille stem in half so you have two 6-inch (15 cm) lengths. Twist the end of one length around the corner of one side of the glasses. Do this again with the second length of chenille stem on the other corner of the glasses. You might want to add a little glue over the twisted chenille-stem ends so they stay in place.
3. Curl the top of each chenille stem into a circle.
4. Glue the lightning bolt on top of the circled end of the chenille stem.
5. With one color of paint, trace around one eye of the sunglasses. Do this again with the second color of paint around the other eye of the sunglasses. With the third color of paint, add a line connecting these two lines of paint in the center.
6. Glue the movable eye in the center between both lenses.

26
Travel
tick-tac-toe game

"Are we there yet?" "How much longer?" Those are two things I'm sure we have all said at one time or another while on a long car trip. It really does seem like forever, doesn't it? Well, there is an old saying that says, "Time flies when you're having fun." So why not enjoy yourself while in the car? It really does seem to take less time if you are doing something. With this project, you can enjoy making the game as much as playing it.

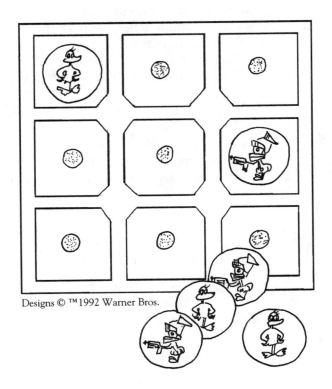

Designs © ™1992 Warner Bros.

materials ☆
- [ ] One 10-inch (25.5 cm) square yellow felt
- [ ] Two 4-inch (10 cm) squares yellow felt
- [ ] 2¼ yards (2 m) blue crinkled ribbon
- [ ] 12-inch-long (30.5 cm) ½-inch-wide (1.3 cm) velcro strip
- [ ] Purple squeezable paint
- [ ] Glue
- [ ] Scissors
- [ ] Assorted colors of markers
- [ ] 8½-inch-x-11-inch (21.3 cm×28 cm) blue card stock paper
- [ ] 2½-inch (6.5 cm) circle stencil
- [ ] Two different characters rubber stamps
- [ ] Black ink pad
- [ ] Ruler

instructions ☆

1. Cut the crinkled ribbon into six 10-inch (25.5 cm) strips and six 3⅓-inch (8.3 cm) strips.
2. Glue four of the 10-inch (25.5 cm) strips around the four edges of the large felt square. Allow a few minutes for the glue to dry.
3. Measure 3⅓ inches (8.3 cm) in from the edge of the felt on one edge. Glue another 10-inch (25.5 cm) strip on this marking. Measure 3⅓ (8.3 cm) inches from this strip, and glue the last 10-inch (25.5 cm) strip.
4. Measure 3⅓ (8.3 cm) inches up from the bottom left corner. Glue a 3⅓ inch (8.3 cm) strip at this point, so that the ends of the smaller strip touch two 10-inch (25.5 cm) strips.
5. Measure up 3⅓ (8.3 cm) inches from this point, and glue another short strip. Continue in the next two columns in the same way. You should end up with nine squares on the felt piece.
6. Now that the tic-tac-toe shape has been made, it is time to paint! Squeezing lightly so that a steady stream of paint comes out, outline the ribbon, painting only on the felt. But don't outline the outside edges. This reinforces the actual tic-tac-toe shape.
7. On all four corners, and then on each of the ribbon intersections in the center, squeeze a large paint dot directly on the ribbon. Try to make the dots as close to the same size as possible.
8. Stroking evenly, paint a small triangle across the corners of the square on the four crosses in the center. Refer to the drawing if you need clarification.

9. With one strip of velcro, cut nine ½-inch (1.3 cm) squares. To make it look better, round off the corners of all these pieces to make nine velcro circles.

10. After removing the adhesive back, put a small drop of glue on each of the velcro pieces, and place them in the center of every square.

11. Put glue around three of the four edges of both the 4-inch (10 cm) felt squares, press them on the back of the board, about ½ inch (1.3 cm) apart to form two pouches. These pouches are used to store the playing pieces when the game is not in use.

12. Using your compass or stencil, trace 12 2¼-inch-diameter (5.6 cm) circles on the card stock paper, and cut them out.

13. Select your two favorite stamps. Ink the stamp, them press hard and evenly. Transfer the design to one of the circles. Try to get the stamp as close to the center as possible. You should stamp six circles with one of your characters and the other six with the other stamp.

14. Carefully color each piece using markers.

15. Cut 12 more circles of velcro, following the instructions in steps 9 and 10. Attach these to the backs of the stamped circles.

27
Seashell mobile

This project and the next one are fun to make from the seashells you collect at the beach. They're great projects to make for gifts, or even for yourself.

materials ☆
- ❏ One 5-inch (12.5 cm) embroidery ring or craft hoop
- ❏ 5 yards (4.5 m) ⅜-inch-wide (.9 cm) double-faced pink satin ribbon
- ❏ Approximately 26 2-inch (5 cm) or 3-inch (7.5 m) seashells
- ❏ One 6-inch-wide (15 cm) clam shell
- ❏ Silicone glue

instructions ☆
1. Wrap the ring with approximately 1½ yards (2.3 m) ribbon. The wraps should be slightly touching each other so the ring is completely covered. Glue the end of the ribbon down.
2. Cut four 12-inch (30.5 cm) lengths of ribbon. Tie one end of one piece to the ring. Tie the other three in the same manner, equally spacing them around the ring.
3. Bring the other ends of all four ribbons together in the center, and tie them in an overhand knot to form a hanging loop.
4. Cut the remaining ribbon into four pieces approximately 27 inches (68 cm), 18 inches (45.5 cm), 15 inches (38 cm) and 12 inches (30.5 cm). These measurements could vary, just have all four different lengths. Glue one end of each piece of ribbon over the ring spaced between the ribbons already attached.
5. Glue the seashells at different places down the ribbon. Glue the large shell on top of the ring.

28
The Gang

We used a total of five shells—one each of cowrie, chula, scallop, green turbo, and snail—to make this cool project. You can represent each one of the members of your family or your friends with a different shell creature. It is amazing how the shells take on personalities when the eyes are added.

THE GANG

materials ☆
- [ ] One 3½-inch-wide (8.8 cm), deep scallop shell
- [ ] Two ¼-inch (.6 cm) moveable eyes (one pair for each shell chosen)
- [ ] 1¾-inch-x-⅜-inch (4.3 cm x .9 cm) piece balsam wood

☐ Thin marker
☐ Silicone glue

instructions ☆
1. Turn the scallop shell upside-down on the table.
2. Glue the various shells you chose on the top and sides of the scallop shell.
3. Glue two eyes to each shell.
4. Write your message on the piece of wood with a marker and glue it to the front of the scallop shell.

Part 7
Back to school

The time has finally come—the time to put all our fabulous summer memories behind us and to face the real world. The time has come . . . to go back to school! This section is filled with projects you can make and wear to school or give as a gift to a friend, brother, or sister. The other kids will go crazy trying to figure out how you make them!

29
Stenciled shirt

The way I see it, if we have to go back to school anyway, why not look good? And what's better than a shirt or sweatshirt you made yourself?! And on top of that, what's better than wearing a hand-designed shirt with the name of your school or special school group on it? In my opinion, there is no better way of sharing your crafting abilities with others than to wear it! And hopefully your newly designed sweatshirt or T-shirt will make going back to (gulp!) school a little more fun!

materials ☆
- ☐ Sweatshirt or T-Shirt
- ☐ Super Silver Color Tool spray or color of your choice
- ☐ Teal Blue Color Tool spray or color of your choice
- ☐ Black squeeze-on paint
- ☐ ½-inch-wide (1.3 cm) masking tape
- ☐ Newspaper (lots of it)
- ☐ Square of cardboard the size of the shirt
- ☐ Plastic wrap

spraying ☆

Prepare an area in a well-ventilated garage or outside for spray-painting. An adult should help you with this step. Choose an area that is not near anything that might be damaged by spray spatters, and cover the work surface with newspaper.

Lay the shirt flat on the newspaper. Cover the cardboard with plastic wrap, and place it between the front and back of the shirt so the paint doesn't soak through. Hold the spray can 12 to 18 inches (30.5 to 45.5 cm) from the shirt. Start spraying off the shirt; then slowly move the spray onto the shirt, and keep going until you are off the shirt again. Use a very light touch. Keep a steady movement; always move the can slowly instead of holding it in one place.

instructions ☆

1. Use masking tape to print the words that will appear on the front and sleeves of your shirt. If you are making a T-shirt, remember that the sleeves are shorter, so long words won't fit. Think of each strip of tape as a stroke of a pencil. For example, the left, right, and center strokes in the letter H are each a separate strip of tape. For circular letters, use squared-off corners instead of curves. (That is why the letter O here looks like a square.) Press the tape onto the shirt. If you don't like the way it looks, simply pull it off and put it where you want it. When you are satisfied with the letters, press the tape down firmly one more time to be sure it is secure so that no paint will seep under it.
2. Spray each color of paint across the front and sleeves of the shirt in a striped pattern. Spray right over the tape. The paint will dry in about 10 minutes. When the paint is dry, peel away the tape to reveal your words. The color of the shirt will show through where the tape was.

3. Use squeeze-on paint to draw decorations anywhere you like on the shirt. Since my shirt is for choir, I drew musical notes. Choose your decorations to tie into the activity or group you are making the shirt for, or just use geometric designs such as circles or lines.

tips ☆　❐　I used Design Master Color Tool sprays. Don't use regular spray paint; it will make your fabric stiff.

30
Decorated book bag

Squeezable, wearable-art paint, felt, and fabric glue work great
when decorating your book bag for school. You can make any
designs you desire. One of the most popular ways is to use your
school's emblem and mascot name and colors.

I went to Northwood Elementary in North Canton, Ohio, and our
mascot name was TIGERS. We used a paw print as an emblem,
which is an easy one to re-create. I made three small circles and

one larger circle from black felt. Then, using the fabric glue, I glued these in a paw-print configuration on the lower half of the book bag.

With white paint, I drew the emblem on the top half and wrote the word TIGERS. Dots of dark blue and white paint completed the design. Use your imagination and have fun as you create a truly unique book bag for school.

31
Light-up sweatshirt

The little lights in this design actually blink off and on. It all works with a special battery pack. You will need to remember to remove the lights before the shirt is laundered each time. After washing the shirt, simply place the lights back into the holes. Your teacher might not appreciate your shirt blinking during class, but you easily can turn the lights off until recess, or just wear the shirt outside of school. Try other designs with these lights besides the one I have drawn. You'll get a lot of attention.

materials ☆
- ☐ White sweatshirt
- ☐ Brush-on paint: pink, yellow, blue, orange, red, & green
- ☐ Squeeze-on paint: yellow, green, purple, & pink
- ☐ ¼-inch-wide (.6 cm) paintbrush
- ☐ Sharp point of scissors or an awl
- ☐ Lightables-brand set of 10 lights
- ☐ Fabric tracing paper or pen

instructions ☆

1. Trace the heart and transfer it to the center on the upper half of the front of the shirt.
2. Trace the I from the pattern and transfer it above the heart.
3. Trace the crayon from the pattern and transfer six of them, placing three on either side of the heart. Use our layout, or try your own.
4. Write the word SCHOOL under the heart and crayons. You can make it neat, or uneven as we have done.
5. Using the paints mentioned above or your own choice of colors, brush the brush-on paint onto the crayons and heart.
6. Outline the crayons, heart, I, and SCHOOL with squeeze-on paint. Allow the shirt to dry.

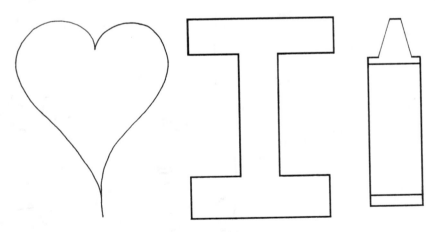

installing ☆
lights

1. Lay the Lightables module on top of the garment. Spread the lights to your desired positions over the design, and make a small marker dot on the fabric where each light will go.
2. Make a small ⅛-inch (.3 cm) opening at each mark with a sharp, round object, such as the point of a sharp pair of scissors or an awl. Ask an adult for help with this.

3. Place the Lightables module inside the garment, and firmly push each light up through the openings. To keep the fabric from unraveling around the light holes during washing, I recommend covering the edges of each light opening with no-fray or with clear nail polish.

4. You may attach the electronic panel to your garment with the hook and loop material, or just let it hang loosely.

5. When the lights are through the openings, slide the enclosed rubber O-rings over each light, and push down firmly against the garment.

6. To operate, just push the button to ON.

32
Handprint magnet

This is a great gift idea for family and friends. They love to watch you grow. It would be interesting to give the same person a handprint each year so that they can compare it with the one you gave them last year!

Billy

materials ☆ ☐ Felt
☐ Pencil
☐ Squeeze-on fashion paint

☐ ½-inch (1.3 cm) magnet strip or circle
☐ Glue

instructions ☆ 1. Place your hand on a piece of paper and trace around it. You could leave the hand this size, or reduce it. Cut this shape from cardboard.
2. Place the hand shape on the felt, and trace it. Cut the hand from felt.
3. Glue the felt hand to the cardboard hand.
4. Use squeeze-on paint to add a dot to each finger and to add your name on the front.
5. Glue the magnet to the back.

Part 8
Halloween

Parties, trick-or-treating, dressing in costumes, and lots of candy—that's what comes to mind when I think of Halloween. I love Halloween, and I know you probably do, too. The designs in this section were created to make the Halloween season more fun. Have a great time!

33
Pom-pom spider

This cute little spider can be a party favor. Or add a barrette if you are a girl, and wear it in your hair!

materials ☆
- [ ] One 2½-inch (6.5 cm) black pom-pom
- [ ] One ½-inch (1.3 cm) tan pom-pom
- [ ] 1½-inch (4 cm) square pink felt
- [ ] Two ⅝-inch (1.5 cm) oval movable eyes
- [ ] Four 12-inch (30.5 cm) black chenille stems
- [ ] Glue

instructions ☆
1. Hold all four chenille stems together.
2. Find the center of this group, and glue the center to the top of the large black pom-pom. Be sure to push the group down into the fluff of the pom-pom to make it stick.
3. After the chenille stems are dry, separate them to resemble legs.

4. Curl the ends of each stem in a circular fashion to resemble feet.
5. Glue the tan pom pom into the center of the large black pom-pom.
6. Glue the two eyes above the tan pom-pom.
7. Cut the teeth from the pink felt using the pattern.
8. Glue these two teeth below the nose.

tips ☆ ❏ Optional barrette variation: Create the spider as listed above but glue it to a spring hair clip.

34
Painted pumpkin

Instead of carving pumpkins this year, why not try painting them?
They will last longer because the process of decomposition is
speeded by carving, and you don't have to carve a painted
pumpkin. Besides, the bright colors give it a real neat look.

materials ☆
- ❏ Medium- to small-sized pumpkin
- ❏ Squeezable paint in black and white
- ❏ Acrylic paint: white, blue, black, & red
- ❏ ¼-inch (.6 cm) flat paintbrush
- ❏ Pencil

instructions ☆
1. Wash and dry pumpkin well before beginning to paint.
2. Draw or trace the facial features from the illustration onto the pumpkin with a pencil. You can follow our design exactly, or you can use your own imagination. Have fun with this design!
3. When painting each area with acrylic paints, you might need a few coats to get full coverage. Wait until one coat dries before painting the second coat on top of the first.
4. First paint the nose with red acrylic paint. Paint the teeth and the outside strip of the eyes with white acrylic. Paint the middle strip of the eyes with blue acrylic, and the center of the eyes with black acrylic.
5. When the paint is dry, outline the mouth, teeth and eyes with black squeezable paint and add dots for the whites of the eyes with white squeezable paint.

35
Halloween painter's cap

Here is a fun design that you can make on a hat you wear all during the Halloween season. Many patterns are given here; use all of them as shown, or choose your favorites.

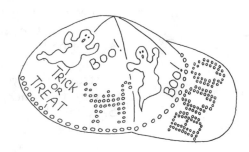

materials ☆
- ❏ Black painter's cap
- ❏ Orange Colorpoint squeezable paint
- ❏ White Colorpoint squeezable paint
- ❏ White iridescent squeezable paint
- ❏ Yellow glow-in-the-dark squeezable paint
- ❏ Regular squeezable paint: orange, blue, & black

instructions ☆
1. Either place the hat snugly on a wig form or tightly stuff it with paper for ease of working.
2. The cat and large BOO on the brim were done with the Colorpoint technique, which is a series of dots of paint that make up the design. Follow the dot pattern shown for BOO and

place this design on the brim of the hat. The illustration will show you the dot pattern for the cat.

3. Using the red and blue squeezable paint, place a row of larger dots around the bottom edge of the hat. Alternate the colors around.

4. Use the remaining patterns shown to decorate the rest of the hat randomly. Put the designs anywhere you choose.

TRICK OR TREAT

BOO!

tips ☆ ❐ It is important to use this brand of paint if you wish to make the design with dots as shown. It is specially formulated to do this.

36
Feather mask

Beads and feathers work together to make this a spectacular
Halloween mask. Try making variations with other beads, paint,
and strips of ribbon.

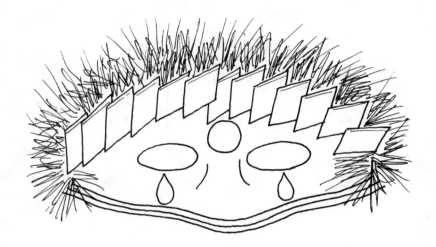

materials ☆
- ☐ Silver half mask
- ☐ 12-inch (30.5 cm) length blue feather garland
- ☐ Twelve 1½-inch (4 cm) assorted-colored diamond mirror beads
- ☐ Two ¾-inch (1.8 cm) blue teardrop-shaped flat-back beads
- ☐ Glue

instructions ☆
1. Glue the feather garland around the top and sides of the mask.
2. Overlap the 12 diamond beads across the top of the mask, gluing them in place.
3. Glue the round bead in the center between the eyes and one teardrop below each eye.

37
Phantom mask

Here is a quick Halloween costume. Simply cut up a half mask as described below, wear a cape and black clothing with a black hat—nothing could be easier!

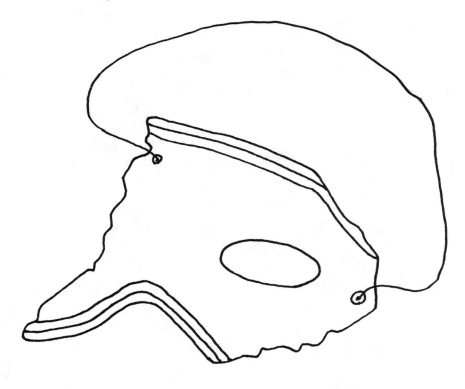

materials ☆   ❏ White half mask
                 ❏ Sharp-pointed scissors
                 ❏ Pencil

instructions ☆ 1. Remove the elastic band from the hole on the left side of the half mask.
2. Draw a jagged line from the bottom of the mask on the left side of the nose, up to the top of the mask at an angle.
3. Cut away the left side of the mask with the scissors.
4. Cut away a little of the mask on the right side above and below the elastic band. Do this in a jagged fashion also.
5. With the point of the scissors make a hole about ½ inch (1.3 cm) from the top of the mask on the left side. Ask a parent for help here. If you have an awl, that works even better.
6. Insert the end of the elastic band, and tie in a knot behind the mask so it won't pull through.

Part 9
Fall & Thanksgiving

Fall is a wonderful time of year. I love the beautiful colors in the trees and the fresh crispness of the air. Thanksgiving is a special time when family and friends gather to give thanks for the many blessings we receive each year. The projects in this section will help you celebrate this season creatively.

38
Leaf shirt

Here is a great way to remember some of the beautiful leaves you gather. Try to select leaves with a wide variety of shapes, sizes, and textures to make this design interesting.

materials ☆
- ❏ Blank T-shirt
- ❏ Leaves with veins
- ❏ Assorted colors of brush-on wearable-art paint
- ❏ 1-inch (2.5 cm) paintbrush
- ❏ Paper towel
- ❏ Rolling pin

instructions ☆
1. Paint the back of a leaf in a color of your choice.
2. Lay this leaf paint side down on the shirt. Place a sheet of paper towel on top of the leaf.
3. Using a rolling pin, very gently but firmly roll over the leaf a few times. Don't get jumpy or try to work too fast because you might move the leaf as you are rolling it, and the impression won't be as crisp. Also be careful the fabric doesn't wrinkle or crease.
4. Repeat steps 1, 2, and 3 over and over until you have as many leaf designs on your shirt as you want.

39
Pinecone turkey

These perky little guys make great favors at the table. Or make several, and place them in the center of the table surrounded by fall leaves as a table decoration.

materials ☆
- ❏ One pinecone
- ❏ Gray or brown construction paper
- ❏ Approximately 24 1½-inch (4 cm) to 2-inch (5 cm) pressed leaves (see project 41 for pressing instructions)
- ❏ Two brown chenille stems
- ❏ Red acrylic paint
- ❏ Yellow acrylic paint
- ❏ Small paintbrush
- ❏ Thin black marker

- ❏ Glue
- ❏ Tracing paper
- ❏ Pencil

instructions ☆

1. Cut three 3-inch (7.5 cm) chenille stem lengths, one 2-inch (5 cm) length, and two 1-inch (2.5 cm) lengths.
2. Glue the 2-inch stem in the center of one of the 3-inch stems so it looks like a T.
3. Bend the other two 3-inch lengths 1 inch from the ends at a right angle, as shown.
4. Glue point A of each piece made in step 3 into the bottom of the pinecone as feet.
5. Glue point A of the illustration centered behind these two to help balance the turkey.
6. Glue the two 1-inch lengths so the middle of the stem falls on point B and C and so one end is glued to each base. The turkey should stand.
7. Then glue the leaves to the bottom (broad side) of the pinecone in a circular fashion.
8. Trace the turkey head from the illustration, and cut it out on construction paper. Glue the head to the front of the pinecone. Draw feather lines with the magic marker, and draw an eye. Paint the beak yellow and the mouth and gaggle red.

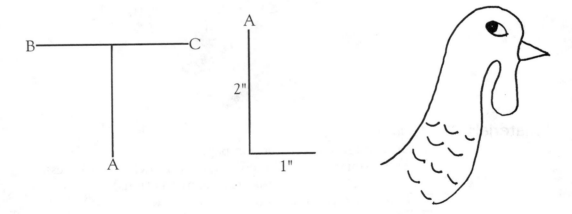

40
Thanksgiving place card

Help out during Thanksgiving and make a place card for each person who will be present at Thanksgiving dinner. Your parents will appreciate your help, and you'll have fun making the project. NOTE: The materials and instructions given here are for one place card.

materials ☆
- ❏ Toilet paper roll
- ❏ Assorted pressed fall leaves (see project 41 for instructions on preparing pressed leaves)
- ❏ Three 1½-inch (4 cm) silk leaves
- ❏ Five ½-inch (1.3 cm) lacquered berries
- ❏ Glue
- ❏ Heavy paper
- ❏ Fine black marker
- ❏ Scissors
- ❏ Wire cutters

instructions ☆ 1. Cut a 1-inch (2.5 cm) slice of the toilet-paper roll
2. Cut a ½-inch-×-1-inch (1.3 cm×2.5 cm) piece of the heavy paper
3. Glue the roll to the heavy paper on its end. You should be able to see through the hole in the center. This will allow the roll to stand.
4. Glue one silk leaf over each end of the hole in the toilet paper roll. One silk leaf should be glued to the top of the roll.
5. Glue pressed leaves on the front and back of the roll to cover it.
6. Write the person's name on the heavy paper, and cut around the name. Glue this to the front of the design on one of the pressed leaves.
7. Cut the wires off the lacquered berries, and glue the berries on the leaves any way you like.

41
Leaf wreath

Gathering leaves in the fall is fun because you can find a huge variety of sizes and shapes. The bright, rich colors are so eye-catching that you will want to save and display these leaves for months to come, and this craft is a perfect way to do that.

materials ☆
- ☐ One 12-inch (30.5) cardboard craft ring
- ☐ Approximately 50 fall leaves in assorted shapes, sizes, and colors
- ☐ Three miniature Indian corn cobs
- ☐ A few pinecones
- ☐ A few pieces of lacquered berries or other decoration
- ☐ One roll paper towel
- ☐ Heavy books
- ☐ Glue

instructions ☆

1. Roll out a few sheets of paper towel. Lay the leaves out one by one, with room around each.
2. Cover the leaves with two sheets of paper towel of equal length.
3. Place more leaves out, cover with two more sheets of paper towel, and continue until all the leaves have been used.
4. Cover the leaves and paper towels with several extremely heavy books. Let this all set as-is for up to two weeks. Then remove the books, throw the paper towel away, and stack the leaves in a shallow box.
5. Glue the leaves around the cardboard ring, overlapping and stacking them randomly as you go around. Completely cover the ring with leaves.
6. Glue the three corn cobs at the base of the wreath and glue the cones, berries, and other decorations randomly over the remainder of the wreath.

Part 10
Christmas & Winter

Besides my birthday, Christmas is my favorite time of year. It is a time when we all gather together, visiting family and friends, decorating trees, making Christmas cookies, and planning special gifts for special people. I've filled this section with ideas for you to make as gifts for family and friends. Have a great holiday season!

42
Star-of-David ornament

Hanukkah is celebrated near the time of
Christmas. Here is a great idea that also makes
a great gift.

materials ☆
- ❏ Six popsicle sticks
- ❏ Deep-blue glittered brush-on paint
- ❏ Paintbrush
- ❏ One 6-inch (15 cm) length ⅛-inch-wide (.3 cm) blue ribbon
- ❏ Six flat-backed ¼-inch-wide (.6 cm) round faceted beads
- ❏ Twelve flat-backed ½-inch-wide (1.3 cm) oval faceted beads
- ❏ Glue

instructions ☆
1. Paint the popsicle sticks with the blue paint. It's best to lay the sticks out on a piece of wax paper or foil first. Paint one side of each of the sticks. When that side is dry, turn the sticks over and paint the other sides.
2. Glue three popsicle sticks into a triangle shape by overlapping and gluing the tips of the sticks. Repeat to form a second triangle.
3. Glue the first triangle on top of the second triangle with the points facing in opposite directions.
4. Bring the ends of the 6-inch (15 cm) ribbon together and glue both ends to the top of the star to form a hanging loop.
5. Glue the beads along the front edge of the popsicle sticks. Place one round bead at each point of the star and one oval bead on either side of the round bead.

43
Reindeer visor

Pretend you are Dasher, Dancer, Prancer, or even the famous Rudolph the Red-Nosed Reindeer with this easy-to-make visor. These instructions are compliments of Talisman of GA, Inc. See the Sources section for contact information; they sell the visors.

materials ☆
- ❏ One white plastic child's visor
- ❏ One 6-inch-×-12-inch (15 cm×30.5 cm) piece brown craft foam OR one 6-inch-×-12-inch (15 cm×30.5 cm) piece brown felt and one 6-inch-×-12-inch (15 cm×30.5 cm) piece poster board
- ❏ One 4-inch (10 cm) square white craft foam or felt
- ❏ One 1½-inch (4 cm) red pom-pom
- ❏ Two 1-inch-wide (2.5 cm) wiggle eyes
- ❏ ½ yard (.5 m) ⅞-inch (2 cm) red plaid Christmas ribbon
- ❏ 1 yard (.9 m) ⅛-inch-wide (.3 cm) red double-faced satin ribbon
- ❏ Two ¼-inch (.6 cm) jingle bells
- ❏ Tracing paper

instructions ☆
1. Trace the patterns for the ears and antlers onto the tracing paper.
2. With the patterns from step 1, cut two antlers from brown felt or foam, two outer-ear patterns from brown felt or foam, and

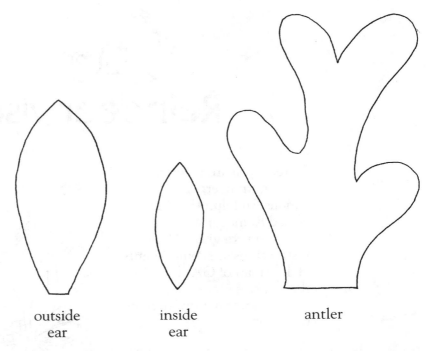

outside
ear

inside
ear

antler

two inner-ear patterns from white felt or foam. If you used felt
instead of foam, also cut two antlers from poster board, and glue
the felt pieces on top of the poster board pieces.

3. Glue the strip of plaid ribbon around the edge of the rim of the
   visor.
4. Glue the bottom of the antlers in their proper position on the
   inside of the visor rim. If you are using felt, it should face
   forward.
5. Glue the inner ears into the center of the outer ears.
6. Glue the ears in front of the antlers on the outside of the visor
   rim, on top of the ribbon.
7. Glue the red pom-pom in the center of the brim of the visor
   near the front edge.
8. Glue one wiggle eye on either side of the pom-pom.
9. Cut the double-faced ribbon into two ½-yard (.5 m) pieces. Tie
   a bow with each, just like you would tie your shoe. Glue one
   bow on top of the other, and glue them next to one of the ears
   of the reindeer.

44
Snowflake ornament

Beads are wonderful to use for ornaments because they catch the lights of the Christmas tree and sparkle and shine. You can adapt and change this idea by using other beads and other colors.

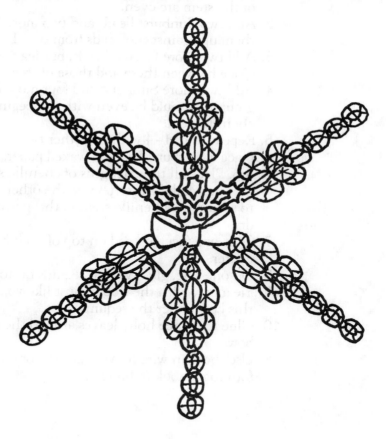

materials ☆

- ☐ Fourteen 18 mm clear Sunburst beads
- ☐ Thirty-eight 6 mm clear faceted beads
- ☐ Three flat-backed green holly beads
- ☐ Two red sequins
- ☐ Three 4-inch (10 cm) white chenille stems
- ☐ One 6-inch (15 cm) length ⅜-inch-wide (.9 cm) red double-faced satin ribbon
- ☐ One 6-inch (15 cm) length thin wire
- ☐ Glue

instructions ☆

1. Insert the chenille stem into four faceted beads, pulling all four to the opposite end of the stem so the bead and the end of the stem are even.
2. Add two Sunburst beads and two more faceted beads, pulling them up against the beads from step 1.
3. Add two more faceted beads, but leave about ½ inch (1.3 cm) space between these and those of step 2.
4. Add two more Sunburst and four more faceted beads. This grouping should be even with the beginning end of the chenille stem.
5. Repeat steps 1–4 with the other two lengths of chenille stem.
6. Place a Starburst bead on waxed paper, and add glue to the top. Place all three lengths of chenille stem on top of the bead in a snowflake pattern. Glue the other Starburst bead on top to secure the chenille stem in this position. Wait until this is dry.
7. Glue one faceted bead on top of each Starburst bead in the center.
8. On one side, glue two red sequins on top of the faceted bead.
9. Tie a bow with the ribbon, just like you tie your shoe. Glue this bow under the sequins.
10. Glue the three holly leaves around the faceted bead above the bow.
11. Use the thin wire to wrap around one end of the snowflake, forming a hook to hang.

45
Starfish Santa

Starfish are wonderful souvenirs of a vacation by the ocean. Sometimes they can be found along the ocean, other times they can be purchased at a shell shop. More and more craft stores around the country are now selling a wide variety of shells. This project is a fun way to make use of them.

materials ☆
- ❏ One starfish, approximately 4½ (11.3 cm) inches wide
- ❏ One ¾-inch (1.8 cm) white pom-pom
- ❏ One 7-inch length (17.5 cm) ⅛-inch-wide white double-faced satin ribbon
- ❏ Acrylic paint: red, white, black, pink, & peach.
- ❏ Small paintbrush
- ❏ Glue

instructions ☆ Follow the drawing and paint:

1. Santa hands and feet - black
2. Fur around wrists and ankles - white
3. Santa hat, shirt, pants - red
4. Fur along bottom of hat - white
5. Fur down center front of suit and along bottom of suit coat white
6. Belt - black
7. Belt buckle - silver

8. Hair and beard - white
9. Face - peach
10. Eyes - black
11. Cheeks - pink
12. Nose, mouth - red

Bring the ends of the ribbon together, and glue them to the top of the starfish. Then, glue the pom-pom on the top of the starfish, over the ribbon ends.

46
Heirloom ornaments

In my family, every year we cut down a tree and put on all the ornaments that we have saved from past years, but there is one special ornament we make. It always has the year written on it, and there is a pocket on the back of the ornament. We spend a minute and write down things we want to remember from the past year. We then fold up our papers and put them into the special pocket on the ornament. It is fun to go back and read about the things we found important in past years.

materials ☆

- ❏ One 3-inch (7.5 cm) wooden embroidery hoop
- ❏ One 6-inch-×-11-inch (15 cm×28 cm) sheet red or green felt
- ❏ One 33-inch (83.5 cm) length red or green crinkled ribbon
- ❏ Four ¼-inch (.6 cm) green holly-leaf faceted beads with flat backs
- ❏ Two ½-inch (1.3 cm) green holly-leaf faceted beads with flat backs
- ❏ Squeeze-on paint: white, red, & green
- ❏ Red or green brush-on paint
- ❏ Paintbrush
- ❏ Glue

instructions ☆

1. Undo the embroidery hoop so there are two separate rings. Place the hoops on waxed paper. Paint both sides of each hoop, allowing the paint to dry between sides.
2. Cut one 3½-inch-×5-inch (8.8 cm×12.5 cm) piece and one 6-inch (15 cm) piece from the felt.
3. Place the smaller felt piece over the lower half of the small inside embroidery hoop.
4. Place the larger piece centered over the same hoop. Place the large, outside hoop over the felt and around the inside hoop. Tighten the screw on top of the large hoop to hold the hoops together. You might need help here. It takes a little strength to screw the hoop over these two layers of felt.
5. Use the scissors to cut away the extra felt from around the outside of the hoop.
6. Cut two 12-inch (30.5 cm) lengths of crinkled ribbon. Glue one piece around the outside edge on each side of the hoop. You either can glue the ribbon down flat, or let it twist and turn the way it normally does.
7. To make a hanger for the ornament, use the rest of the crinkled ribbon. Slip one end of the ribbon under the screw on top of the hoop. Bring the ends of the ribbon together and tie them in a knot. Pull one side of the ribbon until the knot is underneath the screw. Glue the knot to the top of the hoop so it stays.
8. Glue one small holly-leaf bead to the front of the ornament, beneath the knot.
9. Glue one large holly-leaf bead on each side of the small leaf. To make a holly berry, squeeze a large drop of red paint in the center of the leaves. Glue holly-leaf beads to the center top edge of the pocket on the back of the ornament, the same as you did for the front of the ornament. Make a holly berry in the same way.
10. With red or green squeezable paint, write the year on the front, below the holly leaves. With white paint, paint rows of dots beneath the year.

Product credits

The following is a list of products that were donated by their manufacturers for use in the projects in this book. I hope you will find this list useful as you create the crafts in this book. In addition, I would like to gratefully acknowledge the contributions of these manufacturers.

part 1 ☆
Party rubber stamp	Rubber Stampede
Fireworks rubber stamp	Rubber Stampede
Felt markers	Marvy
Curling ribbon	Lion Ribbon Company
Nylon net or tulle	Falk Industries
Rub-off letters	Hygloss Products Inc.
Stick-on stars	Hygloss Products Inc.

part 2 ☆
Picot ribbon	C. M. Offray Inc.
Rub-off letters	Hygloss Products Inc.
Dimensional paint	Tulip
Popsicle sticks	Forster Manufacturing Co. Inc.
Paper doilies	Hygloss Products Inc.
Heart-shaped flat-back beads	The Beadery
Diamond mirror beads	The Beadery
Red webbing spray	Carnival Arts
Suncatcher frame	Kelly's Crafts
Liquid leading	Kelly's Crafts
Liquid glass stain	Kelly's Crafts

part 3 ☆
Dimensional paint	DecoArt
Two-part plastic button	Kelly's Crafts
White greeting card with envelope	Hampton Art Stamps
Bag rubber stamp	Rubber Stampede
Markers	Pentech
Gold ink pad	Hampton Art Stamps
Shamrock-shaped confetti	Z-Barten Productions

part 4 ☆

Felt	The Felters
Pom poms	Aldastar
Puzzle card with envelope	Rubber Stampede
Easter basket rubber stamp	Rubber Stampede
Egg rubber stamp with three ½-inch eggs	Rubber Stampede
Bunny rubber stamp	Rubber Stampede
Grass-cluster rubber stamp	Rubber Stampede
Sun rubber stamp	Rubber Stampede
Colored markers	Pentech
Brown stamp pad	Hampton Art Stamps
Green stamp pad	Hampton Art Stamps
Basket	Wang's
Clear-plastic two-part egg	Wang's
Clear silicone	Creatively Yours Clear Silicone by Loctite
Crafter's Cement	Creatively Yours Crafter's Cement by Loctite

part 5 ☆

Felt	The Felters
Pony beads	The Beadery
Blank doorknob hangers	Rubber Stampede
Teddy bear/moon/stars rubber stamp	Rubber Stampede
Spider stamp	Hampton Art Stamps
Spider web rubber stamp	Hampton Art Stamps
Tasmanian Devil rubber stamp	Rubber Stampede
Paintbrush rubber stamp	Rubber Stampede
Party rubber stamp	Rubber Stampede
Name stamps	Rubber Stampede
Hologram star sequins/confetti	Z-Barten Productions
Brush markers	Marvy
Stamp pads	Hampton Art Stamps
Silicone glue	Creatively Yours Clear Silicone by Loctite
Mickey Mouse rubber stamp	Rubber Stampede
Single-balloon rubber stamp	Hampton Art Stamps
Twisted-paper ribbon	M.P.R. Associates
Acrylic beads	The Beadery
Rub-off letters	Hygloss Products Inc.

part 6 ☆	Stick-on stars	Hygloss Products Inc.
	Curling ribbon	Lion Ribbon Company
	Red and blue floral spray	Design Master
		Color Tool Spray
	T-Shirt form	DecoArt
	Star beads	The Beadery
	Precurled ribbon	C.M. Offray & Son, Inc.
	Squeeze-on paint	Tulip
	Crinkled ribbon	Karen's Creations
	Character rubber stamps	Rubber Stampede
	Silicone glue	Creatively Yours
		Clear Silicone by Loctite

part 7 ☆	Spray dye	Design Master
		Color Tool
	Lightables	Eisenbraun Reiss Inc.

part 8 ☆	Pom-poms	Aldastar
	Felt	The Felter's Co.
	Squeezable paint	Dizzle
	Colorpoint squeezable paint	Tulip
	Masks	Wang's
	Feather garland	Zucker Feather Co.
	Beads	The Beadery

part 10 ☆	Popsicle sticks	Forster Mfg.
	Glittered brush-on paint	DecoArt
	Sunburst and assorted beads	The Beadery
	Visor	Talisman of GA
	Crinkled ribbon	Karen's Kreations

other credits ☆ The manufacturers listed here donated products to me for other projects, which were not used in this book.

	Premade satin bows	C.M. Offray & Son Inc.
	Ribbon roses	C.M. Offray & Son Inc.
	Box-pleated ribbon	Wm. E. Wright
	Squeeze-on fabric paint	Dizzle
	Scenic sand	Activa Products Inc.
	White sneakers	Wang's
	Baseball-style hat	Wang's

Rhinestone beads	The Beadery
Tote bag	Wang's
Hula loops	The New Berlin Co.
Witch stencil	S&S Worldwide, Inc.
Glow-in-the-dark squeezable paint	Tulip

Mail-order sources

The following companies have donated product for use in this book. Check your local craft shop to find these materials. Some of the companies sell through mail-order; others will refer you to someone in your area who carries the specified products. The remainder of the companies sell only to retail craft stores or wholesale outlets. Share the address of these companies with your local shop if it doesn't carry the product you need, and perhaps the shop will be able to order your supplies for you from the company. Happy crafting!

Activa Products, Inc.
PO. Box 1296 DC/SO
Marshall, TX 75671
(903) 938-2224
Products available mail order.

Aldastar
60 Broadway
Brooklyn, NY 11211
Wholesale sales only.

The Beadery
P.O. Box 178
Hope Valley, RI 02832
Wholesale sales only.

Carnival Arts, Inc.
P.O. Box 4145
Northbrook, IL 60065
Wholesale sales only.

DecoArt
U.S. Hwy 150 & 27
Stanford, KY 40484
Write for retail outlet near you.

Design Master Color Tool, Inc.
358 Arapahoe Ave.
Boulder, CO 80302
Wholesale sales only.

Dizzle
One Cape May St.
Harrison, NJ 07029
Wholesale sales only.

Eisenbraun Reiss Inc.
256 Executive Drive
Troy, MI 48083
(800) 762-3108
Call for retail outlet near you.
Falk Industries
569 Broadway
New York, NY 10012
Wholesale sales only.

The Felters Company
Highway 215 & Buffalo Rd
Union, SC 29379
Wholesale sales only.

Forster Mfg. Co.
79 Depot St.
Wilton, ME 04294-0657
Wholesale sales only.

Hampton Art Stamps
19 Industrial Blvd. Dept. DC
Medford, NY 11763
(800) 229-1019
Call for retail outlet near you.

Hygloss Products available mail-order from:
Craft Marketing Connections
Highway K-30 NW
Ireton, IA 51027
(712) 278-2340

Karen's Kreations
2920 Technology Drive
Rochester Hills, MI 48309
Wholesale sales only.

Kelly's Crafts
P.O. Box 219 Dept. CFK
Ross, OH 45014
Send $2.00 for catalog which will be refunded with first order.

Lion Ribbon Company
Route 24, Box 601
Chester, NJ 07930
Retail sales only.

Loctite Corp.
CY Instructions
4450 Cranwood Ct.
Cleveland, OH 44128
Send a long, self-addressed, stamped envelope with a $.52 stamp for free instructions.

MPR Associates, Inc.
P.O. Box 7343
High Point, NC 27264
Wholesale sales only.

The New Berlin Co.
P.O. Box 911
Muskego, WI 53150
Write for retail outlet near you.

C.M. Offray & Son, Inc.
Route 24, Box 601
Chester, NJ 07930
Wholesale sales only.

Plaid Enterprises, Inc.
1649 International Blvd.
Norcross, GA 30091
Write for a retail outlet near you.

Rubber Stampede
Wholesale sales only
Ask for products at your local gift, fabric, and craft store.

S & S Worldwide, Inc.
P.O. Box 513
Colchester, CT. 06415-0513
Write for a retail outlet near you.

Talisman of GA, Inc.
1980 B Parker Ct.
Stone Mountain, GA 30087
Write for retail outlet near you.

Tulip
24 Prime Park Way 4th Floor
Natick, MA 01760
Write for retail outlet near you.

Wang's
4250 Shelby Drive
Memphis, TN 38118
(800) 829-2647
Call or write for a retail outlet near you.

Wm. E. Wright
South Street
West Warren, MA 01092
Write for a retail outlet near you

Z Barten
Call (310) 202-7070, ask for Customer Service.

Zucker Feather Products
512 North East Street
California, MO 65018
Wholesale sales only.

Index